Midnight
at the
Chevron Station

Midnight
at the
Chevron Station

poems and flash fiction
by
Michael Malan

BLUE LIGHT PRESS • 1ST WORLD PUBLISHING

1st WORLD
PUBLISHING

SAN FRANCISCO • FAIRFIELD • DEHLI

Midnight at the Chevron Station

1ST WORLD LIBRARY
PO Box 2211
Fairfield, IA 52556
www.1stworldpublishing.com

BLUE LIGHT PRESS
www.bluelightpress.com
Email: bluelightpress@aol.com

COVER DESIGN
Keri Taff

COVER ART
Adobe Stock

AUTHOR PHOTOGRAPH
Roberta Sperling

FIRST EDITION

Library of Congress Catalog-in-Publication Data

ISBN: 978-1-4218-3572-3

"You can't step into the same river twice."
— Heraclitus
"Of course you can."
— Jay Gatsby

CONTENTS

I. The Red Queen and James Dean

II. Does the Crosstown Bus Run All Night?

III. THE FOREST OF INFINITE WISDOM

I.
The Red Queen and James Dean

New Haven

What we expected when the cows came home:
a friendly feeling about New York,
a quiet evening with Jean-Paul Sartre,
Apollinaire before the lights went out.

A special message from the cafe menu:
leave your personality at home,
get a real job. If you fall in love, elope.
Beware of cookies with fortunes.

When the music stops, buy something
for the monk. If at first you don't succeed,
consider the cat in the rain.

A Week Off

Cars cruise past the Dairy Queen, kids making funny faces
out the back windows of minivans. Every action has a reac-
tion, Luis believes. He has his own private thoughts and, at
the same time, thoughts about other people. Tonight he is
thinking about a boy who jumped off a moving train into a
cornfield as though it were a lake, and the chill that followed
that long winter into April and May. Now he fears for the
lives of others and worries about irrational world leaders.
*Nothing is the same now as it was when we were children and the
sky cannot be pulled down like a curtain.* He recalls the lovely
sunny mornings on his way to work at the train station and
the future as far as he could see was made of slow time. His
dog Bilbo is back by his side after running crazy through the
streets. Later that night he hears engines through his bed-
room window, motorcycles, a whole convoy headed north
toward Sturgis. A week without work and *la vida celestial* is
disappearing from his memory.

Diane

This afternoon, like most others, is set in stone,
the latest super moon an unfinished
symphony in the house of flash fiction,
countless examples of four-way crossings,
searchlight religions, going upriver
with Aquaman, his entourage, another big fish.

Something in the lawn is starting to grow.
St. John's wort or cord grass and rye,
a cathedral of blue horses, stars dancing
on an orange peel, streets tipping
as the moon appears on its great white feet.
Diane was happy, she thought, pretty much.

Just a Glimmer

We were on the road for about two weeks
when the wind hit the fan, the fanbelt broke,

the radiator overheated, and we moved
very slowly, like pomegranates on the suburban

byways. The sky was burning, tomatoes
and strawberries blazing, California one big

conflagration. I got a black eye mowing the lawn.
Now almost everything makes sense.

History, at one time a shadow of something
that might be true, isn't actually repeating itself

as proving us all wrong: the Earth is flat.
On Super Sunday, as I was skating downtown,

past the Sugar Shack, the Guy in the Sky whistled,
and I was stung by a small gleam of logic.

Glacial Republic

1

What we leave when we leave it all behind. Your overdrawn bank account, eiderdown and esoteric studies, everything a puzzle: interstate philosophy or religiosity, depending on your point of view. Astrology, because we take the stars seriously. Moon in Leo, three tornados in one week, floods in West Virginia, a stunning constellation, or wedding vows in Hebrew. The whole thing written down, then torn up and used for kindling. Action repeating itself, mountains disappearing. It's not easy to stand up in a stiff wind and wear your hair like heaven.

2

On campus or up a steep mountain in France—getting lost is cheap entertainment. Tiny alpine forest, Disenchantment Bay, Arrowhead Lake, wherever the maps lead us. Two roads diverging beside a trout-filled stream. Bluegills and pike, the desolate path where Montana meets the grid. Things you see in summer, but not in winter. How the sun ignites your hair as you walk on the beach at Tenerife. Cold skin at dawn, red flowers in blue water, a room with no view, Aunt Betty's big dog. Let's meet at the barbecue, or later, on the avenue of darkness.

Family Portrait

In May, Jenny drove into town and applied for a common-law marriage license at the county courthouse. After she filled out the form, she and her brother Jim and his wife Dorothy posed for a picture in front of the general store. Jenny felt OK, not great, but at least something had been done. That night she watched stars plunge through artificial constellations at a Grange Hall meeting. *There is always something more to be learned about astronomy,* she thought when she saw Mars through a telescope. Days passed and she and Henry came to feel closer after the marriage even though his mind was growing wings and she was thinking about the darkness gathering around her vision of heaven. On the last Sunday in June, she and her sister Rose made tonics, remedies, and cures, and sat in church thinking about refugees in other countries. War seemed far away, like a distant drumbeat. Outside the church, blue glass crystals reflected rainbows across the green Wyoming hills.

A Park Bench in Nevada

A woman stops to talk to her dog. Inspiration at some level is both surprising and funny, each new image illumined by the possibility of reconciliation, or what the March Hare said when the Mad Hatter stopped thinking. The Red Queen and James Dean. Joy has its special message, sunshine when you say hello, a parachute opening like a flower in the sky. When we talk about life and death we are telling the only stories we know. When we talk about Japanese nightingales, we are drawn into fresh bodies of air.

General Delivery

The long journey home after a day or two with Mom,
our shared world view is in trouble: spirit as talisman is
no longer a reoccurring necessity. How brave we are,
each day a special moment, straw on the barn floor, my
horse aghast. Tomorrow implies emptiness or comple-
tion, communion, intoxication, a crowd in bed, locked
up in my home body. In every crescent v, invisible high-
ways cross our world. Rebirth, an alphabet of myste-
rious symbols, helpless muse of deep Christmas striving,
I open the door quietly.

Like a Rose

The spirit will prevail, shift the rhythm
of the body, neurons like branches
uniting rogue waves with memories
of cottonwood, honeysuckle,
and blue fire. *Ooh baby.* Say *yes,*
then follow the rain as it follows the sun.

I felt strangely light-hearted, like
everything would be okay. Someone
had drawn a heart on the back of the door
and inside the heart had written
"Kendra loves Cody." We learned
quickly that things are not as they seem.

Die Kunst ist lang und kurz ist unser Leben.
Or maybe it isn't. I stood for a while,
thinking, speaking softly, then
the warm embrace of silent tears:
the waterfall is like a rose—the sun
and moon and all the stars are breathing.

Crossroads

After the snow speaks and the weeks end,
where shall we go?
Through broken windows
the fragments of trees shine like lanterns
in a purple mist.
The dream of sailing across the ocean
is like lying in a field of clover
as spring unrolls past the river of winter,
the lull of sleep, a gentle breeze,
a red planet
floating in the sky above Li Po's house,

a man in a black cape carrying a rose bush
as a large round shadow
falls on my doorstep.
Offshore, a boulder rises from the ocean
then explodes like a blot of ink
across the horizon.
The wave that follows
is a footprint on the sandy shore.
A cave appears in the forest near the house

where my father lived before he left
the scene of a fatal accident
and drove
to the crossroads
where trees are planted in books.

In his eternal forest, a woman is wading
in a lake of flesh. Two feathers
mark the spot where shame erupts
from her perfect body.
A blue star lights the tip of everything I see.

Ten to One

1. Sending an email is like taking your dog for a walk
    in the logic of numbers.

2. There is nothing less interesting than thinking about
    the moon and the wide Sargasso Sea.

3. The whole affair was rooted in the aftermath of why
    I hope to see you again in the origin of all things.

4. What we were looking for was like creating an illusion
    in the only darkness you can see through.

5. One thing gotten over is like another thing shouting
    its indifference.

6. As we get closer to the source, the period of acceleration
    is reduced by a factor of one, everything else is unreal.

7. En route to the capital city we discovered a narrow path
    through the jungle of museum expeditions.

8. I was home for a while, then I was driving on the freeway
    in the sudden recognition of what might be improbable.

9. I met my dream lover by coincidence in a dark forest
    where I was returning from a happy childhood.

10. She was traveling north as the train was traveling south and songs were being sung in German.

11. On a scale of one to ten, eleven is like starting over with nothing left to chance.

When Nothing Happens

Follow the light as it disappears, or follow the night as it reappears. When you have found the truth, you will have found the still point of any oblique triangle. If you lose your way in the underworld, fear not, the Tigris is close at hand. If the wind speaks riddles, visit the Museum of Natural History. If you find yourself in New York, all is not lost. If there is no room at the inn, bless the junkyard dog. There will be time enough for summer rituals, but not for silent praise. When you approach the Bighorn Mountains, your most recent dream will be broadcast on television. When you get to the final destination, your body is more subtle and your mind has lost weight. When nothing happens, you celebrate the illusion of death.

Ticket to Wait

The fisherman thinks about fish as they swim
upstream. I like to be crazy in the city.
I am grandstanding here in the country.
Not everyone loves me.
Not Pastor Bob who breathes fire on Sunday.
Not the podiatrist who hugged me too close.
Look here, I refuse to be born again.
My bed is a magnet for shock therapy.
Trees, forest, howling moon—the path
through the glen drifts like sand
into another world where stones speak.
I found an apple beside the road—
two worlds colliding. I felt free there,
in the Rockies, with all the walls punched out.
Let me tell you, this house belongs to no one,
not Nicodemus, not the man with X-ray vision.
This space is my space and the train is not often on time.

Far from Michigan

I am tooting the horn in my Oldsmobile
Aurora. My girlfriend wants me to sell
my car, cut my hair short, stop wearing
torn jeans and blue bandanas, trip the
light fantastic. She sits on my chest and
tickles my ears. On the opposite shore
of Lake Superior, people are cheering
and getting all sentimental over me.

The concept: life without Father Luigi,
the sun-burned beach, Roma when
all the girls in my dreams were naked
and the bells of St. Mary's were ringing
a happy tune. Far from Michigan,
a new city is coming down from heaven
like an exclamation point, my perfect
body dragged across the sky like a flag.

Bottom Line

1

In science class Michelle diagrams a weed with epidermal features, blue and red like medieval trade routes. Those roads go on forever, she realizes as the lights dim and a film about outer-space adventurers fills her mind. She remembers a boy in Idaho who rode his horse backwards.

Bottom line: Some explorers, like Marco Polo, needed more than two decades to prove they were living on the wrong planet.

2

Her brother Darren likes to shoot small animals and birds and pretend he's a hunter in Africa. He writes the name of his special girlfriend on a sheet of paper and folds it like an airplane. When he washes dishes, he blows bubbles through a straw he got at Dairy Queen.

Bottom line: His sister ripped his favorite shirt after he pushed her into a lake in Minnesota.

3

Michelle's best friend Sarah got in trouble because she drank too much beer and stayed out late instead of going to a slumber party where everyone was sharing pictures of their parents' weddings. Her dad had all his hair when he got married and her mom looked like a movie star, like a femme fatale.

Bottom line: It's not her party, so she won't do any crying, even if she wants to.

4

Many of the kids at the party look the same, dress the same, think the same thoughts. I want to be more like Sarah, Michelle thinks. Outside the house, across the street, is a cemetery with a tombstone carved like an angel. Inside the house, a man dressed like God is serving brownies and ice cream.

Bottom line: Count to ten, but don't forget who you are. Outside is the new inside.

5

When you fall in love the first time, the edge of the world is out of sight. Michelle's head has grown as large as her house. Birds fly through windows in her brain. People are growing older everywhere, except in the vast universe of Why Not.

Bottom line: When her brother Darren holds his breath, the air speaks volumes. His new T-shirt has a life of its own.

6

Grandpa's '98 Buick LeSabre is parked outside purring like a car salesmen who bought a horse for his stepdaughter. Grandpa is smoking a Lucky Strike, feeling guilty, and imagining he is a famous actor in a play about bus drivers in Tennessee. His wife moved to Japan last summer.

Bottom line: The full moon is a planet inside another moon, like a second universe in the new black hole they discovered in June.

7

The piñata is shaped like a parrot and full of candy, not just fresh Tootsie Rolls and Kit Kats, but leftovers from Halloween. What we expect from the future can't be gathered in our arms or crushed like papier-mâché. When the rain stops, the best ideas are not far behind. We laugh because everything is funny.

Bottom line: Don't try this at home.

Bethesda

Adrienne is walking in Central Park, past the Bethesda Fountain, feeling elated, happy for the first time since her dog died. She is thinking about a man she met while on holiday in the Caribbean. As they sat in lounge chairs beside a heart-shaped pool, he told her he was living with one woman, but loving another. Eventually some mystical experience will awaken him to the realities of life, Adrienne thinks as the New York sky grows dark, shadows fall on the fountain and splash up into the arms of the angel. She studies each of the four cherubs, repeating their names to herself. *Temperance:* Change is more accessible than transformation. We will fuse time and space into one thing and call it afterlife. *Purity:* Form, beauty, harmony, grace. Each moment hovering, calling attention to itself, speaking to the wind, the weather. *Health:* How time unravels, then spools together, then bends and twists back on itself or forward into another day, another year, another time. *Peace:* Remember me. I will always be there for you. In paradise. In your memory. In every white sun and blue pool.

My Week in Fontana

When I see you I want to kiss everyone, hug them
until they are dry—or wet, if they were dry to begin

with. Singing songs of Zion or riding their ponies
on the reservation. This is my collected poems,

my recollected memories. Take me home, busy freeway,
take me home. And then I say: this magazine or that TV

show is like a love song for *tout le monde.* One man or
woman, a treeless prairie, let me be Serbian. If you like

these pastries too much, your best friends will deploy
their rubber hammers and everything set loose will be

nailed down. My lunch, your flowers, the future in star-
darkness. Some poetry is like the dimmest hour. Truth

to tell: I'm ashamed of my mixed feelings, my poor
credit ratings. I am the beast of seven mountains,

the precious glass of damaged hair.

50 States of Mind

1

Like Richard Nixon, I planned to visit all fifty states,
starting first with the tallest towers in New York,
then moving quickly to the star-studded dreamworld
of California. At the back of memory I pitched
a large tent in Wyoming where cowboys were
playing for keeps in the tragedy of personal life.
Each moment replaced by the next, a blunder
here or there, the cosmos suddenly lights up.
"Life is short," the field marshall said as a battle
raged in a twilight forest in Michigan. "Some were
walking in the rain, some were skating on thin ice."

2

In Nebraska the haystacks were burning
like shadows in empty barns. What we learned
in Kentucky embarrasses us now when we argue
about politics. When I go back to Wisconsin,
I say "My name is Yon Yonson and I work
in a lumber mill here." Tell me a story when I see
you again, something racy about Minnesota
or how the truth in Ohio sets you free.
Stars twinkle like parables in a never-ending
voyage. Hawaii, Alaska, don't say I didn't ask ya.

3

I could care less about whetting the whistles
of spring. In Connecticut, foxes don't hang

around chicken coops without passing judgment.
In South Carolina, some are playing with the wind,
some with fire. Everything moves more slowly
in the summer as we wait patiently for the latest
concepts to hatch in New Mexico. All negative
space is shut out: the wilderness of ambition
and frustration, what I felt when the phantom
orchard gave birth to ancient studies.

4

Take my picture in Georgia where the woodlands
become savannahs. A fabulous flowering
tree grows in Louisiana. I can't get enough
of those awesome bedtime stories in Texas.
The fields of Montana are on fire with the
wedding bell blues. Continents drift together,
Washington loves Virginia. I float back and
forth between southern Iowa and *déboisement*,
searching for a secret passage in the back seat
of my soul, that is to say, jumping up and down
as the island method slides firmly into New Jersey.

5

Okay, so I didn't visit every state: Maine was too
far away and Oregon too close. Activity ceased
when I journeyed by stagecoach through the wilds
of Nevada. I beat some drums in Delaware,
lost my hair shirt in Utah. Most of Maryland

was outside the range of infinite capacity
and North Dakota the last stop on the highway
to everywhere. I love how they loved me.
I was a traveling man and made a lot of stops
in Illinois and slept in an irrigation ditch in Kansas.
I left my heart in Florida—I must get back
there sometime soon. The song, not the singer,
not the winebibber: Arkansas, I love your promise.

6

Everything you imagine grows like mixed
feelings in the pleasure of your own company.
The route you take depends on whether you
are traveling in the backwoods of Pennsylvania
or along the golden roads of Vermont.
"Where is my camera, where is my Land Rover?"
When the future comes looking for you, be sure
and hide in the Oklahoma hills. It's a matter
of choice not to notice the obvious, the invisible,
insubstantial, or mysterious: what lies beyond
human sight is the first day of a new experience.

7

Massachusetts is a mouthful, West Virginia
picks me up and takes me home on a crowded
freeway. Almost heaven, New Hampshire.
I am traveling to Rhode Island, the air purple
and hazy; Jimi wants to stand next to your shelter.
All I have left to discover is who I thought
I was when the journey began. Did we linger
too long in Indiana or crash land in an alternate

reality where the young and the brave still live
in the realm of the unreal? "Some were walking
on thin ice, some were skating in the rain."

8

You walk through a mirror like Cocteau
walking through the streets of Mississippi.
All is gold and sapphire in North Carolina.
The weather in Missouri turns warmer in January,
then much colder in March. Scent of autumn
in the air. What we saw and what we couldn't see:
a breeze in the offshore realms of your mind.
The land smiles as the wilderness shines.
The painterly poets in Tennessee are melting
like metaphors on the Boulevard Saint-Michel
and the best view of Notre Dame is blocked
by an overly large monument in Arizona.

9

This morning I was sitting in church thinking
about—forgive me for my active imagination—
a postcard of Freud on Mt. Kilimanjaro.
This sort of thing happens a lot in Idaho,
but not Colorado, so I left my parent's house
in Alabama and moved to South Dakota,
where mountains and rivers are one.
Time and again, past events are reenvisioned,
painted blue and shoved inside our precious
memories. Too late, the expression of hope
ripples in the healthful waters of unexpected
phenomena. I sailed on, through everyday magic.

II.
Does the Crosstown Bus Run All Night?

The Name of the Song

It begins with an old story about two lovers, a deserted house, red flowers, probably impatiens, and a flurry of assurances, where they might go, who they will see, a sense that something or someone is missing. And then there are those events that involve difficult decisions, a cast of characters from a novel they read as college students: a woman who was unfaithful to her husband, unforgiveable really, and yet the husband seemed borish and overly sentimental. Together they move through rooms that seem to be vanishing as they walk, the air outside rushing in behind them from different vistas, configurations of trees, lakes, cabins on a shoreline. September mornings, the promise of some unexpected happening, what you would think was unlikely in any context, but here, in this domestic scene, is frozen in memory. They are dancing to a rock & roll classic from the past and she asks him, "What is the name of this song?" Or, as he is about to drive away, she reaches through the window of his car and touches his beard. He still feels her hand on his face like a kiss, as he drives past vistas of wildflowers, generations of farmers and frontiersmen, his vision shifting from the past to the future. There is something holy about the road.

Dream River

Most of the places I've been are shadows now.
People I don't remember write to tell me
their news. They are changing in unfamiliar
ways. Not growing older so much as falling
asleep in bath tubs or chaining their lovers
to four-poster beds. Lines have been deleted
from their messages, not everyone is ready
to share. Their stories are like dreams, wispy,
old photographs drenched by the sun.

∞

When I close my eyes I hear their voices.
The red and gold plastic radio, *Top of the Pops*
broadcast from Cyprus, my parents sitting
on a leather sofa, smoking and smiling.
I was not comfortable with failure, ignored
by successful relatives, letting the past go,
breathing in hope and magic, expectations
of something better, questions that were
difficult to answer. An exaggerated sense

∞

of delight in hearing how others were making
out on their exotic journeys, then drifting
like an echo between the sheets at night.
And yet, when the past comes back to greet
me, I see glorious adventures everywhere,
wave after wave of vivid memories, stars
and planets drifting in a cosmic ocean.

Those other dreams I try to forget: kicking
dogs and breaking windows, reading *Penthouse*

∞

and pumping iron. I was lost in a forest
of shallow causes, fragments of songs,
a dim light shining in a dog's eyes. I'll drop
some names: Miss HMW, who followed me
home from work on the Palisades Parkway,
Freddy "Boom Boom" Cannon, whose
green eyes twinkled like a kiss at the top
of a Ferris wheel. Change comes. Dreams
vanish in the precious nature of becoming.

Tarot Reading

Vivid memories today. Waiting for the Queen of Hearts to come back from Philadelphia, fucking the High Priestess in the temple garden. My favorite card was the Fool, who, I thought, was free of fear and responsibility, pressures of adulthood, annoying goats and sheep. I wanted to be an adventurer clad in outrageous clothes, holding a rose at the edge of a precipice. I thought I should cast my fate to the wind. But when I drove my car to the mountaintop, it stalled, and the wind kept blowing me back to where I started: endless disappointments, frustrations, and another unfulfilling session with the Hanged Man. His advice was to let the story unfold, let the ending be unexpected, leave one thing behind before moving on to the next thing. "A bleeding corpse pierced by ten swords is not the card of death," he said. "Upside-down, swords are shafts of light." Yeah, and Jesus turned water into grape juice. I wanted the truth. I wanted the world to change so I could be at peace. I was obsessed with obscure texts, elusive lyrics, one-hit wonders, rockabilly wisdom. "My baby done wrote me a letter." Patience, hope, and faith are disappearing idols, I thought as I drove back up the mountain and threw my self-concept over the cliff.

Protestors

On cable news, protestors are talking to reporters, complaining about how much money the rich have stashed away in their stock portfolios. "I work at Walmart," says a young man from Kentucky. "I make $10.75 an hour." A woman is holding a sign that reads, "Where is Robin Hood when we need him?" Others are milling around, making faces at the camera. I thought back to when I was growing up in Fresno and Cinque and his gang were shot by police in L. A. Patty Hearst had been kidnapped and brainwashed, the man on TV said. They showed a picture of Patty in a bank holding an automatic rifle. "Very cool," my brother Seth said, and cocked his finger at me. Patty's dad was named Randolph, my brother told me, and he had a ton of money. "He gave truckloads of chickens to the poor," Seth said, flapping his arms like a bird. The siege lasted several hours. Cinque went out shooting like Butch Cassidy and the Sundance Kid. "The bad guys have all the money," my brother said. "They live on Wall Street and send their goons to kill people." He was smiling. "Some day, they'll get theirs." I wasn't so sure. Our mom and dad kept their money in a bank. "Suckers," my brother said. Today Seth works at Costco, makes $15.50 an hour. He raises chickens and watches Fox News. "It's a living," he says. "Work you develop a taste for." When he hugs me, I feel his muscles tighten. "Let's wrestle, sport," he would have said thirty years ago. Today, a hug is all he wants.

Midnight at the Chevron Station

Here, in the land of you and me only, the natives are untouched by despair, full-bodied encounters with angels from another planet or wandering star. Nothing remains of what you said and did—no surprise, because the radiance has been stowed away for a future excursion. Beyond the arc of relativity displacement, darkness and light are suddenly one with the shadows. A stray dog, a camp made of boards, sleep and desire, a smoking leaf. At night you are barely alive, call of duty, no one says I love you.

Summer Solstice

At the end of the road is another country, a scarf of fog, silence breaking in long waves, the wilderness as it creeps slowly toward the invention of time. Each landscape is a quiet reflection on the subdued chords of powerful images, a delightful metaphor, what we thought about most when the trail ended. Another galaxy, another universe, the harmony of synchronized radio transmitters in Hawaii, Arizona, Mexico, and the Antarctic. A small blue dot in a field of red clover, the moon rising before the sun sets.

Subtropical

Morning, the first memorial, what I wanted when wisdom was a single thing, survival in the Caribbean, a place in the shade, my holy grail. I have no faith in fables or what presumes to fill the empty space. So much of what we say and believe is evolutionary. Here at Sapphire Beach, as the sun sets, we are blessed by the disappearing wilderness, in the last stages of tomfoolery. No earthly surf or shore, red sea belly up, this island paradise collapsing as the winter sun departs in clots of air, moonlight in wicks of trees.

Waiting for a Chinook

So many things found off-putting at first increase
in us as rooms we can live in. The face of silence,

a deep river of absolutely true stories, another
world where the latest journey begins to take on

new meaning: the gospel of everything we hope for,
the unreality of everyday life. And I say: I will always

be your rodeo sweetheart, your bashful buckaroo.
Hold your breath, wait for a chinook, not the tears

of a clown. Let old-school charm be your handsome
neighbor, spirit guide, tenderfoot Jesus, heartbreaker.

Keys to a Different Kingdom

1

An arrow shot through a rainbow, my dog
in jail overnight, Kali and the machine body,

living in the Panhandle while the rain dreams.
The folk art museum closed for remodeling,

the last visitors were from Nova Scotia—
they were in too deep to save themselves.

Prisoner of logic, friend of friendless friends,
I found a Roman coin in a bag of Cracker Jacks.

2

People cheering then booing as six days pass.
Things in this world are reversed, then open

like doors in a show of lust. To be in control
is like a lost city buried in the earth, dawn

in the Mekong Delta, then a closer look at herbal
remedies at the edge of silence. Suddenly

there are shadows surrounding the stadium
and "the amazing nearness" everywhere at once.

3

October, new friends, another life, a bridge
back to the ancient city. A missing sentence

or paragraph, the long walk home after trying
to forget, but the sea won't let you. Moments

of quiet beauty, not the absence of sound.
The key to predictability, another dharmic order.

From the moon new colors, clusters of leaves,
the farm misplaced, tenderness, only the trees sleep.

Trick or Treat

It's Halloween and the moon is full. "Double trouble," Jaylene says. "There may be some ghouls out tonight. Or big, hunky men shapeshifting into werewolves. The world, our culture—it's topsy-turvy. Everything that was nailed down has been set loose." Her face is deathly white and her fingers look like icicles. "Let's talk about something else," I suggest. "The wind on the river or the fog on the mountains. Our tender feelings for one another. The Scary School of Life, the latest Fright Night Installment Plan, or maybe the spooky wizard of Drac-in-the-Box Lane?" We open a party bag of Hershey's Miniatures and eat a few Krackles and Mr. Goodbars. The doorbell rings. Two kids dressed as Spider-Man and Captain America. I hand each a candied apple. "Ooh, sticky," the webslinger says. A large group in dinosaur costumes are coming up next—Jurassic World Fan Club. They take big handfuls from the candy bowl. Dad trails along behind, talking on his cell phone. "What? You're where? What are you doing there?" I look over his shoulder. Someone has knocked down our "We Welcome Everyone to Our Neighborhood" sign. Back inside, Jaylene and I put on our Trump and Biden masks and sit on the couch holding hands. An election is coming soon.

Saying Goodbye

Isaiah was sitting on the floor reading *Meetings with Remarkable Men.* "Gurdjieff didn't think God created the universe," he said. "But He got involved after things got going. It's like God isn't omnipotent, all-powerful, but He plays a role." That made sense to me. "Look at those flowers in Golden Gate Park," I said. "God must have had something to do with that." "Yeah, those flowers are awesome," Isaiah said. We smoked a joint and listened to music on his CD player. Megadeth. Black Sabbath. "I'm going to miss this place," he said. I looked around. It was a pretty dumpy apartment. The windows hadn't been washed in, like, four decades. "When do you think this room was painted?" I asked him. "In the Sixties, I think. Look at those stains on the ceiling." The ceiling was starting to move a little, like the room was breathing gently. "I'm going to Denver," he said, "to see my sister. When it gets cold, I'll come back." I was sad to see him go. Every year one fire dies and another is reborn. Even on the darkest nights, we can see forever.

Urban Ideology

1

Every weekend, all my life,
tiny quakes of leaf and wind,
snow in May, arabesques
of sun and moon, stray cat
on the radiator. Louisiana
bric-a-brac, second marriage,
snowstorm in Liberia, nature
keeps humming, angels speak
to me through a wrinkle
in the cosmos. Some of my
best lines are a kind of bondage.

2

Angola's green bush, a bird
that most likely never existed,
the city is now one hotel
and I inhabit every room.
I am entering life as a star child—
on Sundays, I do a sacred
dance in the foyer. Send me
your dark sidewalk, your
film noir. I am outside
the range of ambivalence—
the wheels stopped spinning
when the lake terror froze.

At the Sunflower Hotel

Backwards or forwards, time past or future,
a view from the heights, torrid nights. At the top

looking up, only stars. Looking down, a trip to Mars.
My two front teeth, a ragged Christmas wreath.

Upstairs, downstairs, do we walk and talk together
or climb a tree where the leaves are shoulder-length?

You get the idea, she said with a smile. Two novels
with one protagonist, the path my neighbor took

to write her book. *Always remember me as I was
then, beautiful, warm, a flash of light on an open sea.*

Inside, outside, I see angels everywhere, except
at Macy's where I work like the devil for whatever.

I can't tell you what it is, but I know it's not mine:
that moment when the universe makes sense,

becomes aligned, and the truth is like a hand
reaching into darkness and turning on The Light.

Out of Focus

In New York, West 82nd Street, Broadway,
fall weather, good vibrations. Winchester
Cathedral, lions at the public library—
I sought refuge from the elemental,
the flowers of young love, leaves falling,
a hymn to women in their bathrobes,
how it all comes back to haunt me.
Castle Rock, Spring Lake, Beauvais.

And then: no free lunch, just up,
down, do the Twist, the Mashed Potato,
eating a sandwich, thinking about eating
a steak, thinking about eating a tiger.
Lean in the shape of lean, the inside
of a lake, winter as a small wave—
in all honesty just a pond in the mind
of an ancient Greek hero. Not Ajax,

the foaming cleanser, tired blood in
the men's room, or a night with Sue Storm
during a tornado. What appeared,
then disappeared. An old story. Bards
sang songs . . . but not so often that
their sopranos were canceled or postponed.
Okay, it was a big deal: sex at first sight.
I get it, the bed shook, the roof

lifted off, people speaking in tongues.
Fortune and fame. Sixteenth century
emblem books, ghost ship expeditions,
a caress not a stone, a force external
to emotion, time wading a frozen river.
And when I left the city, I told them
how I traveled one way, then another,
and found myself wandering.

That Night in El Paso

I HEAR THAT TRAIN

What moves moves. The stars in the rug, the drum beat in the brain, ingredients of enlightened inattention, but in the future, not in the realm of hemming and hawing. Tomorrow, when the buzzing stops, I'll hitch out west and gorge myself on Tonto's special blend. River crossings, wooden rafts, arrows in the masthead. "Don't be a prick-tease," Mom said when she caught us kissing behind the barn. Every now and then, when the silence is oppressive, a train hoots.

TEN YEARS AGO

Faded Angel, Venom and Clay Face, the grand hokey pokey, a city at the bottom of the ocean—or Great Nature in a hollow tree. *Why do you ask? Do the bones speak for themselves?* Another Tupperware party this weekend, some things come right at you out of sync with the Only. Ten years ago, I was in Butte, Montana, strung out on a barmaid. Now I don't drink at all, just read the labels. That night in El Paso, I watched a happy movie on TV, then went to bed. Don't I wish.

Song of Insufficient Reason

Part of the clutter: here only for the translation, preacher
from, or of, the flaming lake, a scene in the flower world,

a dream I no longer recall, my aptitude for power kisses,
secret arrangements with carelessness. Not quite the

panic of last-century divisiveness: adding and subtracting
from what we love most: harmony and *le procès-normal*

in countries you developed a taste for: arid planets in
a distant galaxy, the bones of spaceships in a New Mexico

desert. What's coming is no picnic for the asking: the
eye of the church has gone dim. And around, or within,

the sinuous arts, the doctor paints his green room black.
Freud, Jung, response prevention, poetry and a wall

of silence masking the Heidelberg museum in a cloak of
illumination. Under clear light, the real world becomes

opaque and the joy we felt at Heinrich's bar mitzvah
is riddled with self-deception. It's not what you think,

but how you feel: many of the mountains to the south
are covered with flowers. I have no shadow to lean on.

Terminal Gravity

I meet Kayla at The Peacock for lunch. She's a little bitchy, but that's OK, I love her anyway. She accuses me of watching the TV on the wall above the bar instead of looking at her. I'm not looking at either her or the TV. I'm staring into space, outer space. I see a new black hole forming in the Andromeda Sector. An android waiter appears at my elbow. Kayla orders a bacon burger, French fries, and a pint of Terminal Gravity. I order a soybean burger and V-8 Juice. While we are waiting, she tells me she has gotten an email from "a crazy ex-lover." What should she do? How should she respond? I tell her I don't know. When he returns, the waiter wants to give me the bacon burger. Kayla laughs. I look at the TV: a talking head. No sound. She's enjoying every bite of her bacon burger. Guilty pleasures? Does her husband know? I want to tell her about Jesus. Or the Buddha. *Hari Krishna. Hari Rama.* But I don't. I eat the soybean burger, watch the talking head. His hair is lifting off slowly, like a UFO before it reaches warp speed. The sky over the bar is turning red. Stars are falling on the roof, hitting the street and sidewalk, shattering like Christmas tree ornaments. "Hey," she says, "look at me."

Street/Car

I will not give up my place on the bus, the driver said.
In the Kabbala, the lower world is regarded
as a reflection of the higher.
Jujube, lotus, clover, you must stand
very still when the thicket is blooming.
Others tell the story differently.
Some emphasize the last word or first syllable,
others are paralyzed by immortality.
After the queen returned to her native land,
she was blessed by good fortune.
Take a message, massage the treetops.
Here is a song for a car which is really a flower.

The Vanishing Prairie

1

After my VW broke down in Utah, I was
standing by the road trying to write a poem
of thirty-two flavors, a sort of split-level treatise
on life in America, what Columbus saw
when he arrived in Trinidad, the day calm,
the air palpitating. It was one of those moments
when spiritual growth really takes off.
You buy another car with the insurance money,
an electric vehicle or something more turbo,
and the sun goes on shining. Or it doesn't.
A hard rain beats a tattoo on your disposition.

2

Does form follow function? Everything
is alive, even the pepperoni pizza in the oven.
Not just the clematis or azalea, but a patio lit up
by centuries of heroic action. None could
afford to hide from the pouring rain or pass
on the unloving. *Auch das Schöne muss sterben.*
The tone is the same, even though the reference,
a man and woman conversing on a street corner,
is elusive. The "I" has disappeared or been
replaced with "we." Are we in this together?

3

Against type, you might say, a man (or woman)
in a baggy coat—out here in the hinterlands

everything matters. The wind scratches
its back against the barn. One state of mind
mirrors another: upstate, downstate
are different worlds. The ocean replaced
by slender lakes, ocean vessels by fishing boats:
we cast our nets to the wind. All the happy
memories you enjoyed before have been traded
for momentary silence, a voice from within.

4

We have journeyed thus far and no farther.
What we perceive is only the tail of the tiger.
True, the answers are obscure at first.
It could be that what seems to be a void
is actually a doorway. That moment
when you realize that who you are is who
you will always be is like a mountain road
that peters out on a map of city streets.
Which direction should you take?
Who should you follow? On a dark night
you feel lost and the rivers are too deep to swim.

5

At times we wander beyond the signs pointing
the way toward salvation, before us mirrors
reflecting foreign images, impressions of lands
to the north or south, boys and girls asleep
in hammocks, the temple gate visible from

the next hilltop. The path is narrow
and the buildings on either side unfriendly.
No Avengers or Justice League to rescue us.
Captain America checked out before lunch,
but was charged an extra day. Everyone was
a player. "Does the crosstown bus run all night?"

      6

The loneliness of words, a shield of a greeting,
what I thought about then and what I think
about now: not entirely free of judgement
and reaction, but trained, like my uncle's horse,
to ride the range without overanalyzing the motives
of my master. Even so, time moves slowly,
rivers throb with good intentions and remote
possibilities. Tonight we will share a stall
in the barn, tomorrow be blinded by the bright lights
of a thousand cities. "They were slow in coming,
their voices unassailable from the distant plain."
We are all drifting in the language of summer.

Twilight/Serenade

Pink stars on the seashore. Heading home
after a tender moment in a room full of saints.
My lover touched her face, compliments
bloomed in the air over Berlin. Hibiscus
so blue it shines brightest in amnesia flowers.
The buildings shook—bad days beg the equation.
Mist on the Brandenburg Bridge, the most
dynamic moment in the life of just one
uninhabited planet. Riding in an unmarked car
through majestic mountains, what I see
I cannot believe: twilight on a painted veil.

III.
The Forest of Infinite Wisdom

When We Talk About Science

As I got closer I saw the door in the forest, heard a wall
of sound rising in the distance. A city humming, talking

to itself. My cousin before his dog died and he tripped
on a moonbeam and fell twenty floors into hollow

memory. After the funeral and before the sun turned
around, the wife of the mayor was flying like a brass

band through the teeth of a lion. At the hospital they
have found another use for bandages: electric charges

burning a hole in heaven. We must be ready, Mother said,
for something convincing here on earth, proof of God,

or the loneliness of splendor. When we talk about science
all our senses are disrupted. We put our hands up, but

don't get called. The sign at the end of the street said YES.

Hats Off

What happened next was unpredictable.
My method worked like this:
Two guys were standing on the street
in front of a bar. A dog yawned.
The music was pretty good—
they know how to say yes in Tennessee.

*

O. J. had just hung up his cleats.
He was angry about something
someone had said the night before
at the towering inferno.
Bear Stearns is still in business even so.
I could have been a trial lawyer,
I was so absolutely down-home.

*

In your bed is when things begin
to change. In Texas or Miami, Florida,
the waiting is over.
I want to know how things turned out.
Was the statue cremated in the last act?
Even John Hancock had some place to go.
In Mexico, the cradle of nations
is like a cloud of dreaming birds.

*

I got up late and went downtown
in the freezing light.
There were robots everywhere

and inappropriate remarks
written in the album of unfriendly
democracies. Days passed.
I was trapped between an Indian
flower and the honey of love.
Horses, check them off.

*

On this date in 1944, sex with sailors
was forbidden. I was out of uniform
and the Japanese garden was put on hold.
The truth of being is like a song
set to reconciliation,
life among the Haibun Masters.
Tell me again about the curse of spending
so much time in the realm of empty pavement.

*

You get pretty good at something,
then it disappears. I was not offended
by the Par-Kay floor. I like this apartment
even though I don't live here.
Not everyone is swallowed up in death.
There is no reason to lift the pink straw
to your mouth. The ocean is raging behind it.

*

After I got home, the blind suddenly
received their sight.
There are more people here than I can count.

It does not matter how loud you whisper,
the whole expedition is slowing down
like a gargoyle of fate. Not Taurus
or Capricorn, but the great white hope.

*

After *vendredi, jeudi* was an unremarkable
squeeze. I felt bad, but not bad enough
to readjust the beachfront in my favor.
The man next to me drank black coffee
from a blue cup. It hardly matters.
A fire was burning on top of Old Smoky.

Happy 21st, Happy Hour

1

I am soaking in a hot tub with a woman born blind. Some-
one I don't know is talking on my phone. I go to a pub,
drink a pint, then walk around London whistling like a coy-
ote. I have not slept for a week. My body has its own per-
sonality: annoying and nagging. When I stop breathing,
everyone starts singing.

2

Mystics in Senegal agree that Wheaties is the Breakfast of
Champions. I am like a tree in the middle of Hyde Park. I
do not take the forbidden herb or laugh out loud when the
bong chimes. The bartender's fancy, after a long silence, a
dry spell, is to take his Hedda Gabler and go home.

3

Outside the tavern, the sky is changing colors. Inside the
tavern, a pitcher of beer is like quantum physics. Tranquil-
ity reigns, no prisoners are taken until after the Vulgate ma-
nuscripts. A man with a golden arm is signing autographs
at Barnes & Noble. After a week in Soho, I am still not con-
scious of the body of Christ.

4

I decided not to go there, to that place, where, you know,
nothing happens. I stopped writing about sobriety and in-
dependence and started writing about the hidden face of
the moon. What the mind does and what the body thinks
are like signposts on the Hallelujah Trail. At the foot of my
bed: a clock that has run out of time.

The First Days of Another Era

1

School was closed for a week because of the weather and John of Patmos was kissing the principal's daughter. In the morning, the most painful memories will be revisited—I'll look at pictures in a dark album of faces. I'll be impressed by the parade of giant sea monsters, then I'll fall asleep as Mr. Fantastic wraps his rubber arms around Sue Storm. Eventually peace will be declared and the remains of the day swept away in a great nude extravaganza.

2

Memory churns darkly then pops up like a jack-in-the-box to suggest we are groping in shadows. Let's watch TV in the faded namelessness of another African continent, an earth-sized remnant of Planet X. Being close like we are to the frontiers of knowledge, separated from the big stuff by rivers and mountains, the roots of darkness infect the ocean of preponderance. My whole plan of action was under review, a new message had been written on a flowering plant.

3

I wanted to roam and feel the wind in my hair, stand on the Plain of Jars and play my guitar. It's not possible now to forget what might have been, how aimless wandering soothes the soul like a gunfight, like the last train to Judgement City, mind and spirit suddenly one and the same. So you don't come round any more and I'm left holding the bag, a bundle of raw emotion. Whether living, loving, concluding, or party going, the longest journey is the most productive.

New Year's Eve

Achtung, amigo. Bay Shore Drive.
Empty gestures then an exchange
of wampum in the primal village.
Ahoy to the greenback visitors.

An alien base outside the orbit
of bodies, planets, people gyrating,
dancing by the pool. Church bells
ringing, a witness to popular songs,
my x-ray personality.

I came here all at once, as a matter
of fact, like nature presupposing
a digital timepiece. Everyone we
know and love is sleeping.

Obsession

My hand against a tree, the weight
of a thousand leaves. Carbon from air,
the illusion of oxygen hybrids, what
I lost overnight in the forest.

Email or *émail,* outdoors at the Élyseé,
a sign in Deutsch: *We want more.*
At the dark edges an old story: a girl
with two cows, revolutionary fervor.

Each day a special moment, straw
on the barn floor, my horse aghast.
And, in the distance, two towers burning.

Clarity

Light, the comfort of frost and shade,
avenue of rebirth, the city of vanishing
shadows, an old Chevy parked on
a beach, only a few feet from oblivion.

Biological, psychological, the moon
born again in a flower-shaped cloud.
I stopped reading your mind when
large animals appeared in the forest
of infinite wisdom.

Starlight, starshine. Let's find some new
words for danger, ambush; the sign
on the wall says *dharma*.

In the Realm of Here and Now

1

Sitting in the first row, I see small planets orbiting the speaker's head. It's all happening in a different time frame, the old man says, one landscape is no more *puissant* than the next. Hawaiian fescue is just another invasive species, Poa annua on the run. Luminosity is not something you attain overnight; it's a byproduct of a monk's immediate gratification. Once crossed, the bridges begin to disappear. Everything grows old quickly, then fizzes out.

2

Waking up in a foreign city is like forgetting who you are in the middle of another life. A platoon of men and women working hard to create a new system, the great army of mandates notwithstanding. It will be up to my neighbor Alana and her hairy beau to navigate the middle ground between hunky first nation and pie à la mode. Two are not necessarily better than one, especially when the woman upstairs is a better kisser.

3

Since graduation I've mostly slept on the couch, read a few novels, but found no practical solutions for helplessness. Some days, like today, I feel like heading south, down Rio Grande way—I'll board a freighter in the Gulf, find something new and unusual. It will be pink, newborn, an island in the Galápagos. I will find a big turtle there, in the Galápagos, a ring of holy fire, a halo in the sky, the secret weeping of a broken stone.

Spring Break

1

At the *malheur* outer reaches, the absent-minded
are smiling. You can live for a long time
in sun and shadow, but eventually the special
architecture kicks in and the family farm
is sold for a pittance. Quality is dispersed
equally as the next journey grows shorter,
loud music just a footnote in the symphony
of super powers. At night other sounds
are heard as you drive out to sea. The lighthouse
is closed, locked up like the ghost of electricity.

2

Flagged, pulled over on the upper freeway
of thought, broken like Humpty Dumpty
after a great fall, names are dropped,
more than you can count, and poems
buried under an avalanche of exposition.
Through the fog of indecision we become aware
of the imbalance at the center of depravity.
No awards are passed out. You stand
on a stage thinking your head is too large
and the rush of emotion is like a fender bender
in the final stages of acceleration.

3

Mesmerism has its place in the strong feelings
we have for our neighbors and friends:

Bob, who jumps through metaphors,
and Ursula with her "bright, shining light."
We can't cross a lake more than once
without experiencing some turbulence
around their inertia. I sometimes think
these quirky times are worth a laugh.
Declining days are deliberately avoided:
let's fight crime and press flesh with the French.

4

When we travel by car, as we do most Sundays
en plein air, the avenues seem to stretch out
beyond the soul's habitation. To complain
about the past is like the story of the princess
who rejected the handsome prince and fell
into a trance when the clock struck evil.
It was easier not to grow up than to think
outside the tank: mulberry trees line boulevards
between here and the voice of anger.
What hurts most is not the first query,
but the unreliable subtext in the fourth dimension.

5

In frontier novels, tears are shed, but eventually
the cowpoke mentality prevails and all the folks
sit down to a hearty meal. The grandchildren
are allowed to speak for a few moments
before Grandpa shares stories about "the war

in Albany." Who we are now and who we were
before are suddenly the same thing. You know,
a tree falls in Brooklyn, then rolls downhill
into a complicated trance. After she moved in,
la grande dame threw a party for darkness.
She was not bothered by infidelities—
she knew that Trojan women are built to last.

      6

After I wash dishes, I take Dog for a walk.
Every grownup I see looks stunned—
our camouflage proved useless. In those days,
a good time could be had, if not by everyone,
at least the native space was unsettled.
Truth, in the sense of how things really work,
is no longer an open question—my brain,
after a week in outer space, lights up
like a neon sign and another brutal pigment
is added to the dull sky of tomorrow.
What I saw as I walked back to the dorm
was like a dream unfolding.

Something to Write Home About

The brain doesn't care who is coming and going, the
seasons where tone is a voice in a parallel universe,

or that particular moment when Dad believed he could
survive as a stick figure among the hungry. In time,

the street people disappeared, but not before the
members of their glee club joined the secret march to

Magic City, and the lights in the cavern blew themselves
out. Noted for its unexpected forays into turbulence,

the quick fix was unlocked, and the radical fan boys
brought up through the ranks of soundless tundra,

the various subspecies arranged in hairline fractures,
a wall of subtext separating my favorite comic books

from do-it-yourself, jerk-the-penguin, railroad funnies.
Things too unreal to be from western New York,

a note of panic in the whispering village.

Heat/Wave

Ninety-five degress last night and the city stopped talking.
What we are doing in the darkness is like a tree hanging on
the wind between your mind and the painted mountains.
After the call ended I thought about history books and lakes
of ice. I will not crawl on my knees across the Atlantic. Two
women are playing tennis and the earth is like a white ball
in the space between two symphonies. I am speaking to you
now from the Bill of Rights. What I saw when I looked inside
the book of stars: I am never on time.

What Happened at Midnight

The secret of the old mill was still a question mark as we drove along Lake Shore Road. Time is like poetry, dance music, a healthy lifestyle, the philosophy of impermanence. Frank touched the brakes and the road turned to ice.

*

We stopped our car in front of a dilapidated old house on a cliff above Barmet Bay and rang the doorbell. A gloomy young man answered and invited us in. He showed us his collection of broken blades, then vanished through a secret panel.

*

While the clock ticked, we searched the fireplace for a clue in the embers. All we found were melted coins and a twisted claw. We ran outside and discovered footprints under the kitchen window and a weird mark on the back door.

*

A message arrived on our short-wave radio: "Something strange has been sighted on Skull Mountain. If you get there first, don't forget the Sinister Signpost." We jumped in our roadster and drove out of town toward Skeleton Rock.

*

How brave we were. We drove and drove, past the Hidden Harbor and out beyond the Crisscross Shadow and The Sign of the Crooked Arrow. The air doubled back on itself and rain seeped in through the detachable hardware.

*

"Oh, Frank," I said. "Maybe we should call Dad for help. He's a famous detective." Frank wasn't so sure. He knew what Dad would say. "For better or worse, serve the greater good, write it down or forget it. Grow up, get a 'real' job."

*

A hooded hawk flew overhead and a yellow feather drifted down from heaven. Across the bay, we could see a flickering torch where the phantom freighter had been docked. What happened at midnight will always be a mystery.

Absent Without Malice

1

Justine asks if she can stay the night, but leaves a few hours later on a ferry. I follow in a small craft through choppy seas. Each window in her new home has a different point of view. She is waiting for a man I don't know, though he seems familiar, like someone I should know, like someone I have seen before. He is looking out a window, not her window, another window, at a playground where children are laughing and running in circles around an ancient statue. In time, the playground will be obscured by fog rolling in from the bay and the bay will be abandoned by all but the sturdiest ships.

Between the ocean and the coastline is the supposition
of an empty house. Your hand in front of your face
is a signal that the sky is vanishing.

2

The back door is open and another woman, an older woman, is reading a book about love. In this city there are no libraries, just a few hickory trees and silence in the corridors of power. Justine adored the mayor's chief of staff until he left the city for personal reasons. Her bathtub has been replaced by a *cenoté* and a river is no longer running through it. This is the point on the map where several highways converge and the word "understanding" has been submitted for reevaluation. The effects of my dream last night have dissipated. I am standing outside her apartment trying to read the address.

I feel like I could live anywhere. Toronto, San Francisco,
the North of England. I could stow my possessions
in her attic, wait for a bus to leave the city.

3

I am wearing a suit that has not been pressed. My pants
are stained, my feet damp. Water everywhere, but not rain
or ice. In this city, weather is hard to predict. Some days
the street people are friendly and the memories of their
favorite pantomimes photogenic. I will pray for a new re-
lationship when my lover's ship leaves the port and the
port drifts back to the center of my being. What happens
next is no longer a secret. Together we will climb a moun-
tain and shout hosannas to our friends on the other side
of the valley. She will stop for a burger at the chalet, then
race downhill like a gazelle.

I read the same sentence twice. If you are coming here
to be with me—please, please don't come.

4

The tomb looks smaller from a distance, from offshore,
from the middle of the ocean. Camera in hand, in a small
boat, I find it soothing to rearrange the words that have
been replaced by cardboard cut-outs. The monuments
here and in all the countries to the east are like stars on a
perfect night in mid-December. This is something like the
divine—it hurts so much. On my pillow, tears, but I don't
feel angry. Let's just say that my shadow obscures the
prison doctor's face. Before the clock strikes twelve, I am

in Brisbane sitting across from a woman who knows more than I do about everything.

Twenty-four thousand miles later, in the house
of forgetfulness, I remember a missing detail.

5

The colors of today are melting into the rivers of tomorrow. At first it seems like a blessing, but then, after a moment of reflection, it resembles the earth moving every which way, the secular world repeated in the memory of one hand clapping. This will only hurt for a second, the doctor says, as spears are thrown through the glass doors of a single rose. When they replay my life story, I will listen to their voices as they echo the wind through a broken tulip. These sleights of hand are considered outside of what we think, pro or con, about the marvelous light. When you return from a long journey, familiar landscapes are put on hold.

Some part of the past seems unfamiliar, like a dark
blue flower on the edge of my bathtub. From earliest
times, wooden ships set sail for unknown waters.

6

Along the shore, sailors are reappearing where, at one time, there were only forgotten dreams, a rough beast slouching through the halls of Congress, winter convulsing in back-alley Detroit. People are laughing when they should be serious. Every morning, without pleasure, I will forget the handshakes. It doesn't matter if the Ferlinghettis are away from home—the lonesome prairie is closed for reconditioning. Time is not something we can depend on. What stands for romance is like a new novel breathing. My eyes are closing at the same time as the rainbows are fading.

When I returned later, the house was empty. She had gone outside and found the landscape she loved best.

7

Peace in the valley, not harmony in Valhalla. We were hiking home through fields of bread crumbs. The way was dark, stormy, and tinted with marmalade. I sat by the river as the flowers of nativity tormented the ancient Greeks. Not long after, shadows fell out of style and the blue heron tattooed on my back flew away. We have no other recourse, the chiropractor said, but to approach the divine with an open mind. True enough, the collapse of prophecy and revelation is represented by Jason and the Argonauts. We consider it a tonic in the aftermath of another dangerous adventure.

In my new country, the flag of hope is a candle in the forest. Stars are like windows in trees.

Poems and flash fiction in this book
previously appeared
in the following publications:

New American Writing: "Hats Off," "My Week in
    Fontana," "Crossroads"
Plainsongs: "Something to Write Home About"
Grist: "Song of Insufficient Reason"
Chicago Quarterly Review: "Glacial Republic"
Sugar House Review: "Ten to One"
The Adroit Journal: "Bottom Line"
SALT: "The Vanishing Prairie"
Meridian: "Tarot Reading" and "The Name of the
    Song" (co-winners of the 2024 Editor's Prize),
    "When Nothing Happens"
New World Writing: "A Week Off," "Family Portrait,"
    "Bethesda," "Protestors"
Lake Effect: "Trick or Treat," "Terminal Gravity,"
    "Saying Goodbye"
The Summerset Review: "Obsession"
Crab Creek Review: "Summer Solstice"
Twelve Mile Review: "Heat/Wave"
Puerto del Sol: "Absent Without Malice"
Village Voices: "What Happened at Midnight"
All the Men Came and Danced: "Like a Rose,"
    "Waiting for a Chinook"

About the Author

Michael Malan was born in Missoula, Montana, and "educated" at Antioch College and Cornell University. Each year, students at Antioch studied six months on campus in Yellow Springs, Ohio, and worked six months in diverse locales. During the six years Malan was a student at Antioch, he lived and worked in New York City; Chicago; San Francisco; Washington, D.C.; Columbus, Ohio; Clear Lake, Michigan; Shoshoni, Wyoming; Sunnyvale, California; and Wounded Knee, South Dakota.

In 1999, Malan and Peter Sears founded a small press, Cloudbank Books, in Corvallis, Oregon. Their first book was *Millennial Spring: Eight New Oregon Poets*. *Cloudbank,* a literary journal (cloudbankbooks.com), was launched in 2008. Malan currently serves as editor.

He is the author of three books from Blue Light Press: *Overland Park* (poetry and flash fiction, 2017), *Tarzan's Jungle Plane* (flash fiction, 2019), and *Deep Territory,* (poetry, 2021). His work has appeared in *Epoch, Cincinnati Review, Tampa Review, Washington Square Review, Grist, Denver Quarterly, Poetry East, Hayden's Ferry Review, Potomac Review,* and many other journals.

www.ingramcontent.com/pod-product-compliance
Lightning Source LLC
Chambersburg PA
CBHW032024090426
42741CB00006B/728